REALLY EASY GUITAR

CHRISTMAS CLASSICS

22 SONGS WITH CHORDS, LYRICS & GUITAR GRIDS

ISBN 978-1-5400-9738-5

Visit Hal Leonard Online at
www.halleonard.com

Contact us:
Hal Leonard
7777 West Bluemound Road
Milwaukee, WI 53213
Email: info@halleonard.com

In Europe, contact:
Hal Leonard Europe Limited
42 Wigmore Street
Marylebone, London, W1U 2RN
Email: info@halleonardeurope.com

In Australia, contact:
Hal Leonard Australia Pty. Ltd.
4 Lentara Court
Cheltenham, Victoria, 3192 Australia
Email: info@halleonard.com.au

Angels We Have Heard on High

Traditional French Carol
Translated by James Chadwick

First Note

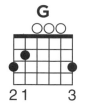

G   D   D7   E   Am   C

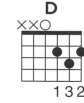 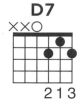 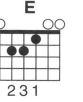 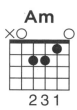

VERSE 1

Moderately

| G | | D | G | | | D7 | G |
Angels we have heard on high, sweetly singing o'er the plains.

| | D | G | | | D7 | G |
And the mountains in reply, echoing their joyous strains.

CHORUS

G E Am D G C D7 G   D
Glo   -   ria in excelsis Deo.

G E Am D G C D7 G   D G
Glo   -   ria in excelsis De - o.

VERSE 2

| G | | D | G | | | D7 | G |
Shepherds why this jubilee, why your joyous strains prolong?

| | D | G | | | D7 | G |
What the gladstone tidings be which inspire your heavenly song?

REPEAT CHORUS

VERSE 3

| G | | D | G | | | D7 | G |
Come to Bethlehem and see, Him whose birth the angels sing.

| | D | G | | | D7 | G |
Come adore on bended knee, Christ the Lord, the newborn King.

REPEAT CHORUS

Away in a Manger

Words by John T. McFarland (v.3)
Music by James R. Murray

First Note

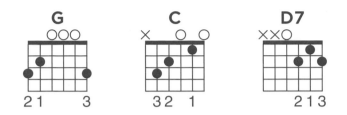

VERSE 1

Moderately

G   C   G
Away in a manger, no crib for a bed,

   D7   G
the little Lord Jesus laid down His sweet head.

   G   C   G
The stars in the sky looked down where he lay.

   D7   G   C   D7 G
the little Lord Jesus, asleep on the hay.

VERSE 2

   G   C   G
The cattle are lowing, the baby awakes,

   D7   G
but little Lord Jesus, no crying He makes.

   G   C   G
I love thee, Lord Jesus, look down from the sky

   D7   G   C   D7 G
and stay by my cradle 'til morning is   nigh.

VERSE 3

   G   C   G
Be near me, Lord Jesus; I ask Thee to stay

   D7   G
close by me forever, and love me, I pray.

   G   C   G
Bless all the dear children in Thy tender care,

   D7   G   C   D7   G
and take us to heaven, to live with Thee there.

Coventry Carol

Words by Robert Croo
Traditional English Melody

First Note

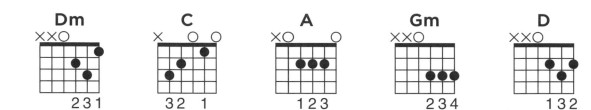

VERSE 1

Moderately

Dm   C A Dm Gm Dm
Lullay, thou little tiny child. By, by, lully, lullay.

  C   Gm A Dm Gm D
Lullay, thou little tiny child. By, by, lully, lullay.

VERSE 2

Dm   C A Dm Gm Dm
Oh, sisters too, how may we do, for to preserve this day?

  C   Gm A Dm Gm D
This poor youngling, for whom we sing by, by, lully, lullay.

VERSE 3

Dm   C A Dm Gm Dm
Herod the king, in his raging, charged he hath this day.

  C   Gm A Dm   Gm D
His men of might, in his own sight, all young children to slay.

VERSE 4

Dm   C A Dm Gm Dm
That woe is me, poor child for thee! And ever morn and day,

  C   Gm A Dm Gm D
for thy parting neither say nor sing by, by, lully lullay!

Deck the Hall

Traditional Welsh Carol

First Note

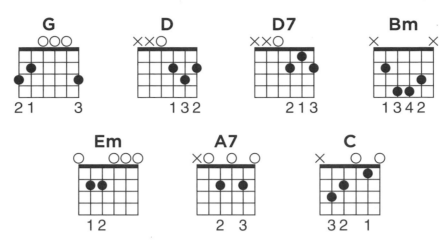

VERSE 1

Moderately

```
G                          D          G   D7  G
Deck the hall with boughs of holly; fa, la, la, la, la, la, la, la, la.

                     D       G   D7  G
'Tis the season to be jolly; fa, la, la, la, la, la, la, la, la.

D            G       Bm    Em    A7   D
Don we now our gay appael; fa, la, la, la, la, la, la, la, la.

G                      C       G   D7  G
Troll the ancient yuletide carol; fa, la, la, la, la, la, la, la, la.
```

VERSE 2

```
G                          D          G   D7  G
See the blazing yule before us; fa, la, la, la, la, la, la, la, la.

                         D       G   D7  G
Strike the harp and join the chorus; fa, la, la, la, la, la, la, la, la.

D            G       Bm    Em    A7   D
Follow me in merry measure; fa, la, la, la, la, la, la, la, la.

G                      C       G   D7  G
While I tell of Yuletide treasure; fa, la, la, la, la, la, la, la, la.
```

VERSE 3

```
G                          D          G   D7  G
Fast away the old year passes; fa, la, la, la, la, la, la, la, la.

                         D       G   D7  G
Hail the new ye lads and lasses; fa, la, la, la, la, la, la, la, la.

D            G       Bm    Em    A7   D
Sing we joyous, all together; fa, la, la, la, la, la, la, la, la.

G                      C       G   D7  G
Heedless of the wind and weather; fa, la, la, la, la, la, la, la, la.
```

The First Noël

17th Century English Carol
Music from W. Sandys' Christmas Carols

First Note

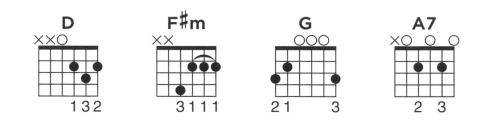

D   F#m   G   A7

VERSE 1

Moderately slow

```
D      F#m  G       D
The first Noël, the angel did say,

      G         D                    A7   D
was to certain poor shepherds in fields as they lay.

       F#m     G          D
In fields where they lay keeping their sheep,

      G         D           A7 D
on a cold winter's night that was so deep.
```

CHORUS

```
   D   F#m  G  D
Noël, Noël, Noël, Noël,

G         D          A7  D
born is the King of Is - ra - el.
```

VERSE 2

```
   D      F#m  G    D
They looked up and saw a star

      G       D          A7     D
shining in the East, beyond them far.

       F#m     G          D
And to the earth it gave great light

   G       D          A7   D
and so it continued both day and night.
```

REPEAT CHORUS

VERSE 3

    D   F♯m   G   D
And by the light of that same star,

    G   D   A7 D
three wise men came from country far;

      F♯m   G   D
to seek for a King was their intent,

    G   D   A7 D
and to follow the star wherever it   went.

REPEAT CHORUS

VERSE 4

    D   F♯m   G   D
This star drew nigh to the northwest,

    G   D   A7 D
O'er Bethlehem it took its rest;

      F♯m   G   D
and there it did both stop and stay,

    G   D   A7 D
right over the place where Jesus lay.

REPEAT CHORUS

VERSE 5

    D   F♯m   G   D
Then entered in those wise men three,

    G   D   A7   D
full reverently upon their knee;

      F♯m   G   D
and offered there in His presence,

    G   D   A7 D
their gold, and myrrh, and frank - in - cense.

REPEAT CHORUS

Go, Tell It on the Mountain

African-American Spiritual
Verses by John W. Work, Jr.

First Note

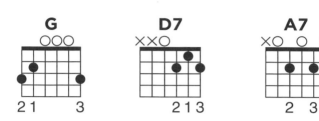

CHORUS

Moderately

G   D7   G
Go tell it on the mountain, over the hills and ev'rywhere.

                                           D7   G
Go tell it on the mountain that Jesus Christ is born.

VERSE 1

      G   D7   G
While shepherds kept their watching o'er silent flocks by night,

                                 A7   D7
behold, throughout the heavens, there shone a holy light.

REPEAT CHORUS

VERSE 2

      G   D7   G
The shepherds feared and trembled when, lo! above the earth

                             A7   D7
rang out the angel chorus that hailed our Savior's birth.

REPEAT CHORUS

VERSE 3

      G   D7   G
Down in a lowly manger, the humble Christ was born,

                     A7   D7
and God sent us salvation that blessed Christmas morn.

REPEAT CHORUS

I Heard the Bells
on Christmas Day

Words by Henry Wadsworth Longfellow
Music by John Baptiste Calkin

First Note

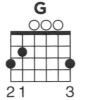 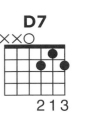 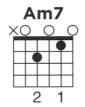 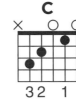 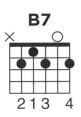 

G   D7   Am7   C   B7   Em

VERSE 1

Moderately fast

G   D7   G   Am7   D7
I heard the bells on Christmas day, their old familiar carols play

G   C   G   B7   Em   G   D7   G
and mild and sweet the words repeat, of peace on earth, goodwill to men.

VERSE 2

G   D7   G   Am7   D7
I thought how as the day had come, the belfries of all Christendom

G   C   G   B7   Em   G   D7   G
had rolled along th'unbroken song of peace on earth, goodwill to men.

VERSE 3

G   D7   G   Am7   D7
And in despair I bowed my head: "There is no peace on earth," I said,

G   C   G   B7   Em   G   D7   G
"For hate is strong, and mocks the song of peace on earth, goodwill to men."

VERSE 4

G   D7   G   Am7   D7
Then pealed the bells more loud and deep: "God is not dead, nor doth He sleep;

G   C   G   B7   Em   G   D7   G
The wrong shall fail, the right prevail, with peace on earth, goodwill to men."

VERSE 5

G   D7   G   Am7   D7
Till ringing, singing on its way, the world revolved from night to day.

G   C   G   B7   Em   G   D7   G
A voice, a chime, a chant sublime, of peace on earth, goodwill to men!

God Rest Ye Merry, Gentlemen

Traditional English Carol

First Note

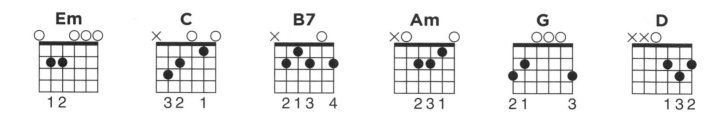

VERSE 1

Moderately slow

   Em   C   B7
God rest ye merry, gentlemen, let nothing you dismay,

   Em   C   B7
for Jesus Christ our Savior was born on upon this day,

   Am   G   Em   D
to save us all from Satan's power when we were gone astray.

CHORUS

   G   B7   Em   D
O tidings of comfort and joy, comfort and joy;

   G   B7   Em
O tidings of comfort and joy.

VERSE 2

   Em   C   B7
In Bethlehem, in Jewry, this blessed Babe was born,

   Em   C   B7
and laid within a manger upon this blessed morn;

   Am   G   Em   D
to which His mother Mary did nothing take in scorn.

REPEAT CHORUS

VERSE 3

       Em   **C**   **B7**
From God our Heav'nly Father, a blessed angel came;

       Em   **C**   **B7**
and unto certain shepherds brought tidings of the same;

       Am   **G**   **Em**   **D**
how that in Bethlehem was born the Son of God by name.

REPEAT CHORUS

Hark! The Herald Angels Sing

Words by Charles Wesley
Altered by George Whitefield
Music by Felix Mendelssohn-Bartholdy

First Note

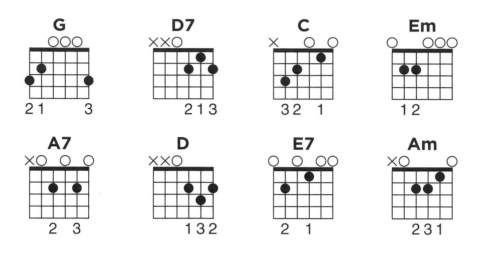

VERSE 1

Moderately fast

G   D7 G C   D7   G
Hark! the herald angels sing, "Glory to the newborn King!

          Em A7 D   A7 D
Peace on earth, and mercy mild, God and sinners reconciled!"

G   C   D7 G   C   D7
Joyful, all ye nations, rise, join the triumph of the skies;

C   E7 Am   D7   G
With th'angelic host proclaim, "Christ is born in Bethlehem!"

C   E7 Am   D7 G   D7   G
Hark! the herald angels sing, "Glory to the newborn King!"

VERSE 2

G   D7   G   C D7   G
Christ, by highest heav'n adored, Christ the everlasting Lord;

                   Em   A7   D   A7   D
Late in time behold Him come, offspring of the virgin womb.

G   C   D7 G   C D7
Veiled in flesh, the Godhead see: Hail, th'incarnate Deity;

C   E7   Am   D7   G
Pleased, as man, with men to dwell, Jesus, our Emmanuel!

C   E7   Am   D7   G   D7   G
Hark! the herald angels sing, "Glory to the newborn King!"

VERSE 3

G   D7   G   C   D7   G
Hail, the heav'n-born Prince of Peace! Hail, the Son of Righteousness!

                   Em   A7   D   A7   D
Light and life to all He brings, ris'n with healing in His wings.

G   C   D7 G   C   D7
Mild He lays His glory by, born that man no more may die,

C   E7   Am   D7   G
Born to raise the sons of earth, born to give them second birth.

C   E7   Am   D7   G   D7   G
Hark! the herald angels sing, "Glory to the newborn King!"

It Came Upon the Midnight Clear

Words by Edmund Hamilton Sears
Music by Richard Storrs Willis

First Note

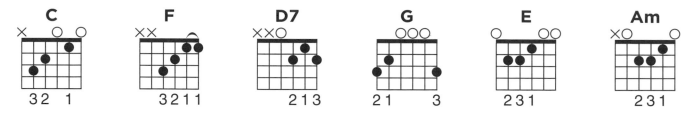

VERSE 1

Moderately slow

    C   F   C   F   D7   G
It came upon the midnight clear, that glorious song of old,

       C   F   C   F   G   C
from angels bending near the earth to touch their harps of gold.

       E   Am   G   D7   G
"Peace on the earth, goodwill to men from heaven's all gracious King."

    C   F   C   F   G   C
The world in solemn stillness lay to hear the angels sing.

VERSE 2

    C   F   C   F   D7   G
Still through the cloven skies they come with peaceful wings unfur,

    C   F   C   F   G   C
and still their heavenly music floats o'er all the weary world.

   E   Am   G   D7   G
Above its sad and lowly plains, they bend on hovering wing.

    C   F   C   F   G   C
And ever o'er its Babel sounds the blessed angels sing.

VERSE 3

    C   F   C   F   D7   G
O ye beneath life's crushing load, whose forms are bending low,

     C   F   C   F   G   C
who toil along the climbing way with painful steps and slow.

    E   Am   G   D7   G
Look now for glad and golden hours come swiftly on the wing.

    C   F   C   F   G   C
O rest beside the weary road and hear the angels sing.

Jolly Old St. Nicholas

Traditional 19th Century American Carol

First Note

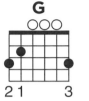   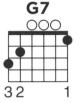 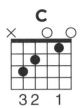 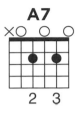

G   D7   Em   G7   C   A7

VERSE 1

Moderately fast

G   D7   Em   G7
Jolly old Saint Nicholas, lean your ear this way.

C   G   A7   D7
Don't you tell a single soul what I'm going to say.

G   D7   Em   G7
Christmas Eve is coming soon, now, you dear old man,

C   G   D7   G
Whisper what you'll bring to me; tell me if you can.

VERSE 2

G   D7   Em   G7
When the clock is striking twelve, when I'm fast asleep,

C   G   A7   D7
down the chimney broad and black, with your pack you'll creep.

G   D7   Em   G7
All the stockings you will find hanging in a row.

C   G   D7   G
Mine will be the shortest one, you'll be sure to know.

VERSE 3

G   D7   Em   G7
Johnny wants a pair of skates; Susy wants a sled.

C   G   A7   D7
Nellie wants a picture book, yellow, blue, and red.

G   D7   Em   G7
Now I think I'll leave to you what to give the rest

C   G   D7   G
Choose for me, dear Santa Claus. You will know the best.

Jingle Bells

Words and Music by J. Pierpont

First Note

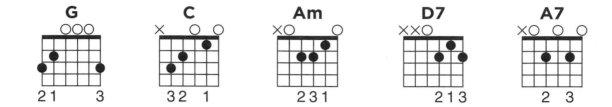

VERSE 1

Moderately fast

G   **C**
Dashing through the snow, in a one-horse open sleigh,

Am   **D7**   **G**
o'er the fields we go, laughing all the way.

                                                              C
Bells on bobtail ring, making spirits bright,

             Am   **G**   **D7**   **G**
what fun it is to ride and sing a sleighing song tonight! Oh!

CHORUS

G
Jingle bells, jingle bells, jingle all the way.

C   **G**   **A7**   **D7**
Oh, what fun it is to ride in a one-horse open sleigh!

G
Jingle bells, jingle bells, jingle all the way.

C   **G**   **D7**   **G**
Oh, what fun it is to ride in a one-horse open sleigh!

VERSE 2

G   C
A day or two ago, I thought I'd take a ride,

  Am   D7   G
and soon Miss Fanny Bright was seated by my side.

                                                               C
The horse was lean and lank, misfortune seemed his lot.

  Am   G   D7   G
He got into a drifted bank and we, we got upsot! Oh!

REPEAT CHORUS

VERSE 3

G   C
Now the ground is white. Go it while you're young,

  Am   D7   G
and take the girls tonight and sing this sleighing song.

                                                              C
Just get a bobtail bay, two-forty for his speed,

  Am   G   D7   G
then hitch him to an open sleigh and crack, you'll take the lead! Oh!

REPEAT CHORUS

Joy to the World

Words by Isaac Watts
Music by George Frideric Handel
Adapted by Lowell Mason

First Note

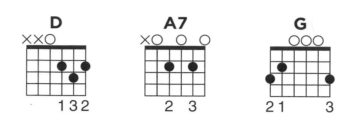

VERSE 1

Moderately fast

D   A7 D   G   A7   D
Joy to the world! The Lord is come; Let earth receive her King;

Let ev'ry heart prepare Him room, and heav'n and nature sing,

   A7   D   A7   D
and heav'n and nature sing, and heav'n and heav'n and nature sing.

VERSE 2

D   A7 D   G   A7   D
Joy to the earth! The Savior reigns; Let men their songs employ;

While fields and floods, rocks, hills and plains repeat the sounding joy,

   A7   D   A7 D
repeat the sounding joy, repeat, repeat the sounding joy.

VERSE 3

D   A7 D   G   A7   D
No more let sin and sorrows grow, nor thorns infest the ground;

He comes to make His blessings flow far as the curse is found,

   A7   D   A7 D
far as the curse is found, far as, far as the curse is found.

VERSE 4

D   A7 D   G   A7   D
He rules the world with truth and grace, and makes the nations prove

the glories of His righteousness and wonders of His love,

   A7   D   A7 D
and wonders of His love, and wonders, wonders of His love.

O Christmas Tree

Traditional German Carol

First Note

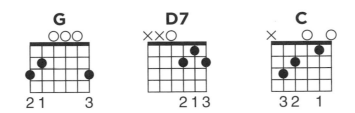

VERSE 1

Moderately

G   D7   G
O Christmas tree, O Christmas tree, you stand in verdant beauty!

                                               D7   G
O Christmas tree, O Christmas tree, you stand in verdant beauty!

                  C   D7   G
Your boughs are green in summer's glow, and do not fade in winter's snow.

                                             D7   G
O Christmas tree, O Christmas tree, you stand in verdant beauty!

VERSE 2

G   D7   G
O Christmas tree, O Christmas tree, much pleasure doth thou bring me!

                                               D7   G
O Christmas tree, O Christmas tree, much pleasure doth thou bring me!

                  C   D7   G
For ev'ry year the Christmas tree brings to us all both joy and glee.

                                             D7   G
O Christmas tree, O Christmas tree, much pleasure doth thou bring me!

VERSE 3

G   D7   G
O Christmas tree, O Christmas tree, thy candles shine out brightly!

                                             D7   G
O Christmas tree, O Christmas tree, thy candles shine out brightly!

                  C   D7   G
Each bough doth hold its tiny light that makes each toy to sparkle bright.

                                             D7   G
O Christmas tree, O Christmas tree, thy candles shine out brightly!

O Come, All Ye Faithful

Music by John Francis Wade
Latin Words translated by Frederick Oakeley

First Note

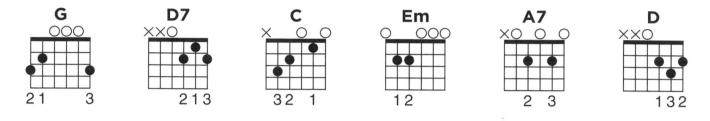

VERSE 1

Moderately

```
     G              D7     G     C    G  D7
O  come,  all  ye  faithful,  joyful  and  triumphant,

     Em   A7   D                    A7      D
O  come  ye,  o  come  ye  to  Beth - le - hem.

     G     D7    C    G    D         Em      D
Come  and  behold  Him,  born  the  King  of  angels.
```

CHORUS

```
     G
O  come  let  us  adore  Him,

                         D
O  come  let  us  adore  Him,

     C          A7  D   C
O  come  let  us  adore  Him,

G     D     G
Christ     the  Lord.
```

VERSE 2

G   D7 G   C   G D7
Sing choirs of angels, sing in exul - ta - tion,

Em A7 D   A7   D
Sing, all ye citizens of heav - en above.

G D7 C G D Em D
Glory to God in the highest.

REPEAT CHORUS

VERSE 3

G   D7   G   C   G D7
Yea, Lord, we greet Thee, born this happy morning.

Em A7 D   A7   D
Je - sus, to Thee be all glo - ry giv'n.

G D7 C G D   Em   D
Word of the Father, now in flesh appearing.

REPEAT CHORUS

O Holy Night

French Words by Placide Cappeau
English Words by John S. Dwight
Music by Adolphe Adam

First Note

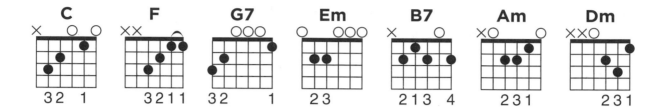

VERSE 1

Moderately fast

C   F   C
O holy night, the stars are brightly shining,

          G7   C
it is the night of the dear Savior's birth.

        F   C
Long lay the world in sin and error pining,

    Em   B7   Em
till He appeared and the soul felt its worth.

 G7   C
A thrill of hope, the weary world rejoices,

 G7   C
for yonder breaks a new and glorious morn.

Am   Em   Dm   Am
Fall on your knees! O hear the angel voices!

 C G7 C F C   G7   C
O night divine, O night when Christ was born!

 G7   C F C G7   C
O night, O ho - ly night, O night divine!

VERSE 2

```
C                         F        C
Truly He taught us to love one another,

                            G7       C
His law is love, and His gospel is peace.

                              F         C
Chains shall He break, for the slave is our brother,

           Em          B7         Em
and in His name all oppression shall cease.

     G7                C
Sweet hymns of joy in grateful chorus raise we,

     G7          C
let all within us praise His holy name.

Am          Em       Dm              Am
Christ is the Lord, O praise his name forever!

     C    G7     C    F    C  G7          C
His pow'r      and glo - ry ev - er more proclaim!

     G7          C    F    C  G7         C
His pow'r and glo - ry ev - er more proclaim!
```

O Little Town of Bethlehem

Words by Phillips Brooks
Music by Lewis H. Redner

First Note

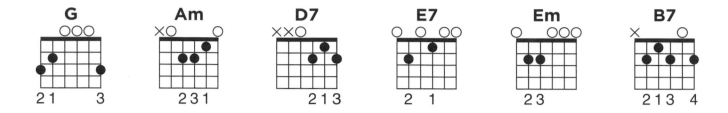

VERSE 1

Moderately fast

  G   **Am**   **G**   **D7**   **G**
O little town of Bethlehem, how still we see thee lie.

         E7   **Am**   **G** **D7**   **G**
Above thy deep and dreamless sleep, the silent stars go by.

  Em   **B7**   **Em**   **B7**
Yet in thy dark streets shineth the everlasting light.

  G   **Am**   **G** **D7**   **G**
The hopes and fears of all the years are met in thee tonight.

VERSE 2

  G   **Am**   **G**   **D7 G**
For Christ is born of Mary, and gathered all above,

        E7   **Am**   **G**   **D7**   **G**
while mortals sleep, the angels keep their watch of wond'ring love.

  Em   **B7**   **Em**   **B7**
O morning stars, together proclaim the holy birth,

  G   **Am**   **G**   **D7**   **G**
and praises sing to God the King, and peace to men on earth.

VERSE 3

G   Am   G   D7   G
How silently, how silently the wondrous gift is giv'n.

E7   Am   G   D7   G
So God imparts to human hearts the blessings of His heav'n.

Em   B7   Em   B7
No ear may hear His coming, but in this world of sin,

G   Am   G   D7   G
where meek souls will receive Him still, the dear Christ enters in.

VERSE 4

G   Am   G   D7   G
O holy Child of Bethlehem, descend to us, we pray;

E7   Am   G   D7   G
cast out our sin and enter in; be born in us today.

Em   B7   Em   B7
We hear the Christmas angels the great glad tidings tell;

G   Am   G   D7   G
O come to us, abide with us, our Lord Em - manu - el.

Silent Night

Words by Joseph Mohr
Translated by John F. Young
Music by Franz X. Gruber

First Note

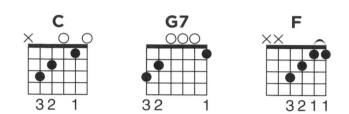

C   G7   F

3 2 1   3 2 1   3 2 1 1

VERSE 1

Moderately

C   G7   C
Silent night, holy night. All is calm, all is bright.

F   C
Round yon Virgin Mother and Child.

F   C
Holy Infant so tender and mild,

G7   C   G7   C
sleep in heavenly peace. Sleep in heavenly peace.

VERSE 2

C   G7   C
Silent night, holy night. Shepherds quake at the sight.

F   C
Glories stream from heaven afar,

F   C
Heavenly hosts sing Alleluia,

G7   C   G7   C
Christ the Savior is born! Christ the Savior is born.

VERSE 3

C   G7   C
Silent night, holy night. Son of God, love's pure light.

F   C
Radiant beams from Thy holy face

F   C
with the dawn of redeeming grace,

G7   C   G7   C
Jesus Lord at Thy birth. Jesus Lord at Thy birth.

Up on the Housetop

Words and Music by B.R. Hanby

First Note

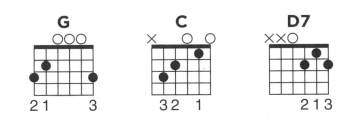

VERSE 1

Moderately fast

G   C   G   D7
Up on the housetop reindeer pause, out jumps good old Santa Claus.

G   C   G   D7   G
Down through the chimney with lots of toys, all for the little ones, Christmas joys.

CHORUS

C   G   D7   G
Ho, ho, ho! Who wouldn't go? Ho, ho, ho! Who wouldn't go?

                               C   G   D7   G
Up on the housetop, click, click, click, down through the chimney with good Saint Nick.

VERSE 2

G   C   G   D7
First comes the stocking of little Nell. Oh, dear Santa, fill it well.

G   C   G   D7   G
Give her a dolly that laughs and cries, one that will open and shut her eyes.

REPEAT CHORUS

VERSE 3

G   C   G   D7
Look in the stocking of little Will. Oh, just see what a glorious fill!

G   C   G   D7   G
Here is a hammer and lots of tacks, whistle and ball and a whip that cracks.

REPEAT CHORUS

We Three Kings of Orient Are

Words and Music by John H. Hopkins, Jr.

First Note

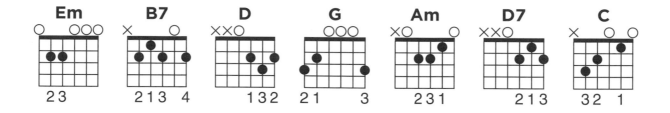

VERSE 1

Moderately fast

Em	B7	Em	B7	Em

We three kings of Orient are bearing gifts we traverse afar.

D	G	Am	B7	Em D7

Field and fountain, moor and mountain, following yonder star. O,

CHORUS

G	C	G	C	G

star of wonder, star of night, star with royal beauty bright.

Em	D	C	D	G	C	G

Westward leading, still proceeding, guide us to thy perfect light.

VERSE 2

Em	B7	Em	B7	Em

Born a King on Bethlehem's plain. Gold I bring to crown Him again.

D	G	Am	B7	Em D7

King forever, ceasing never over us all to reign. O,

REPEAT CHORUS

VERSE 3

Em   B7 Em   B7 Em
Frankincense to offer have I. Incense owns a Deity nigh.

      D   G   Am   B7   Em D7
Prayer and praising, all men raising, worship Him, God most high. O,

REPEAT CHORUS

VERSE 4

Em   B7 Em   B7   Em
Myrrh is mine; its bitter perfume breathes a life of gathering gloom;

      D   G   Am   B7   Em
Sorr'wing, sighing, bleeding, dying, sealed in the stone-cold tomb.

REPEAT CHORUS

We Wish You a Merry Christmas

Traditional English Folksong

First Note

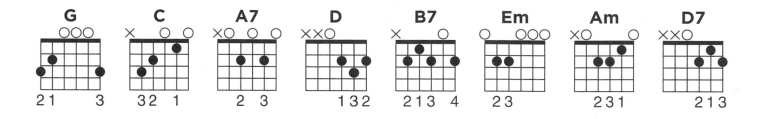

VERSE 1

Moderately fast

G	C	A7	D

We wish you a Merry Christmas, we wish you a Merry Christmas.

B7	Em	Am	D7	G

We wish you a Merry Christmas, and a happy New Year.

CHORUS

G	D	A7	D7

Good tidings we bring to you and your kin.

G	Am	D7	G

Good tidings for Christmas and a happy New Year.

VERSE 2

G	C	A7	D

Oh, bring us a figgy pudding, oh, bring us a figgy pudding.

B7	Em	Am	D7	G

Oh, bring us a figgy pudding, and a cup of good cheer.

REPEAT CHORUS

VERSE 3

```
        G                    C              A7             D
We  won't  go  until  we  get  some,  we  won't  go  until  we  get  some.

        B7                   Em             Am          D7  G
We  won't  go  until  we  get  some,  so  bring  some  out  here.
```

REPEAT CHORUS

REPEAT VERSE 1

What Child Is This?

Words by William C. Dix
16th Century English Melody

First Note

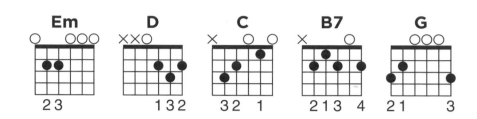

VERSE 1

Moderately slow

    Em   **D**   **C**   **B7**
What Child is this, who, laid to rest, on Mary's lap is sleeping?

    Em   **D**   **C**   **B7**   **Em**
Whom angels greet with anthems sweet, while shepherds watch are keeping?

CHORUS

    G   **D**   **Em**   **B7**
This, this is Christ the King, whom shepherds guard and angels sing.

    G   **D**   **Em**   **B7**   **Em**
Haste, haste to bring Him laud, the Babe, the Son of Mary.

VERSE 2

    Em   **D**   **C**   **B7**
Why lies He in such mean estate where ox and ass are feeding?

    Em   **D**   **C**   **B7**   **Em**
Good Christian, fear, for sinners here the silent Word is pleading.

REPEAT CHORUS

VERSE 3

    Em   **D**   **C**   **B7**
So bring Him incense, gold, and myrrh, come peasant, king to own Him;

    Em   **D**   **C**   **B7**   **Em**
The King of kings salvation brings, let loving hearts enthrone Him.

REPEAT CHORUS